JUNK YARD DOGS

poems

DAMIEN FLORES

West End Press

PO Box 27334

Albuquerque, NM 87125

www.westendpress.org

 Published with the generous support of the City of Albuquerque's Urban Enhancement Trust Fund

Body type set in Bembo. Headings set in Ephesus. At the poet's request, words in Spanish have been set in Roman type. Speech is represented with italics.

CONTENTS

For Mama,

for Grandma,

for Grandpa

ACKNOWLEDGEMENTS

"El Cuento de Juana Henrietta" was previously published in *El Palacio*.

"A Warning for Driving the Wrong Way" was previously published in *Malpaís Review*.

"Elegy for Johnny Tápia" was previously published by *Duke City Fix*.

"The Heights" and "A Dollar Three-Eighty" were previously published in *El Cuento de Juana Henrieta*, published by Destructible Heart Press.

¡Órale raza! Here's my brown soul!

Little Joe y La Familia

I became a poet in church.
Knelt beside Grandma
every day of Lent
every year.
I learned to speak loud
from the pulpit.
The child lector,
my voice shook like a candle flame
at the serpent's mouth
beneath the Blessed Mother's foot
as I read the daily scripture
and the people listened.
In that church, I learned to memorize poems
as I learned to memorize prayers, oraciones
we sang my auntie
at her funeral.
Here I learned the stories
of the saints I was named after:

> San Lorenzo's charred innards
> pulled from his bones,
> stuck to the gridiron
> as the Romans roasted him
> alive;
>
> Damien's rotted fingers
> strumming his guitar,

singing salvation songs
beside the lepers of Molokai;

San Antonio's mercy
for those lost on Earth;

San Francisco, the protector of animals,
who knew the forest's solitude
was proof that God was not cruel
enough to banish us from paradise
completely.

In that church,
I learned to read music.
We chanted alabados and the rosary
in Spanish, set to the centuries-old melodies
the Indians of Mexico hid in the psalms,
to ensure their gods would not die.

In that church
my first poems came
in the silence of the night watch
on Holy Thursday.

My mind strayed
'til midnight, once I
was all out of prayers
and all out of sins.

There was no wind the day Juana battled the machine.
Smoke rose from the stacks of the downtown tortilla factory
slow as the wrinkled and steady hands.
Las viejitas, cocineras
whose fingers were callous as the spirits of their mothers.
They were the assembly line of ancient faces.

They worked for coins off their husbands' wages.
Mothers of the New Deal
labored their bones, dull
with the factory whistle at dawn.

Harina y manteca
became the skin on their palms.
Fifty pounds of flour each dark morning,
as their grip stung with salt grains and leavening.

Tortillas rounded like the suffered
crown of the God carved in the altar,
their God hung above the stove.
Round rolling pins cut from cedars
smoothed with hidden splinters in the hands,
and dough rose before the sun.

This morning hung bitter in Juana's mouth
when the women found machines
on the floor where they once stood.

Here are your replacements,
the boss growled like rusting metal,
There's no work here. I want you all out.

And the ancient faces gazed like forgotten saints
they once prayed to.

Some cursed the foreman's name,
their fists clenched tighter than the gears
in the machine that took their jobs.

But Juana didn't move,
she stood steel-heavy and her wrinkles ran fierce
like flooding arroyos when she said,
I'm faster than any damn machine.

The engine fired,
conveyor belt rolled tamales,
each an exact copy of the last.
Juana took the table beside. Handful of masa.
Cornhusk hidden in her skin.

She spread masa, carne, y chile.

Each glide of her hand
like wiping tears from her daughter's face,
wiped sweat on the back of her fist.
Her salt, a blessing of food at the table.

But she knew it didn't matter if she'd beat the machine.
She'd gone like so many Mexicanas,
rotting like nopales beneath a tractor's heels,

just as the men's backs were replaced
with forklifts and backhoes.

But an engine does not name its children
after a passing rain cloud
does not brush dead leaves from headstones,
and never learned the recipe from her grandmother's tongue.

The machine fired,

la masa, la carne, el chile, la oja
       wrapped like the bandana of Juana's hair
la oja, la masa, el chile, la carne
       bled the crevice of the hands
el chile, la oja, la carne, la masa
       her husband buried in the Philippines
la carne, la masa, la oja, el chile
       her daughter's birth cries
la oja, el chile, la masa, la carne
       her shadow on her wedding day
el chile, la masa, la carne, la oja
       became the peasant maid's machete.

As the engine sang the death of the laborer's breath,
the foreman's eyes never left Juana's face
when the machine slowed down.
Smoke and motor oil snaked the air
and the conveyor stopped.

Juana crushed the last tamale, her voice like a snake's
venom in the chile, *Bésame fundio*
malagracido, sonso viejo estúpido.
¡Toma las tamales y póntelas dentro de tu culo, pendejo!

Her shadow stained the floor where she stood.

The next day, the machines unloaded,
the women manned the controls
but Juana never showed for work.

They said she joined the army.
Maybe opened a restaurant.
Some said she became a corn plant
rooted in burning soil.
But really, none of them knew.

Still their throats all burn from the steam,
the gears grind off and rust in their dreams,
their mouths still dry when they say
the name of the woman and sing legends of the day
Juana Henrieta made tamales against the machine.

My cousin married in the spring.
Our last great family wedding.

The American Legion Dance Hall
was not prepared
for a guest list of 400.
Catered by none other than my grandma.
Music by Al Hurricane,
Al Hurricane Jr.
and their 40-member band.
And with an open bar?
Shit, we should'a sold tickets.

Everyone was there.
Every primo, compadre,
in-law, vecino, jefito y jefita,
tío & tía,
nino & nina,
nana & nono.

And you don't know
who's related to who.

Because New Mexican family trees
are sprawling forests. Thick bosques
with branches tangled in scandal
and leaves like loose tongues;
my family loves to talk shit.

But tonight, everyone came
to laugh and to dance.

The last time we all were alive.
I was thirteen
and I hated weddings.
Years of forced two-stepping
with my aunties swinging me
around like I was the mop
they danced across the kitchen floor
to the rancheras
on the radio.

89.1 KANW New Mexico Music:
The soundtrack of Saturday morning housework.

I blame my mama
for all the school dances
I stood wallflower,
while the vatos and the jocks
got all the girls,
and left me wondering where
I went wrong going right.
But this wedding, this music,
this was my chance
and she was my girl.

Morenita,
red manzana smile.
Her dress, snug like the lace glove
on the bride's hand. She had to be
on the married-in side.
God would not be so cruel.

Then a choir of trumpets
struck a tune as old as the flowers,
and the old Hurricane sang
"Flor de las Flores,"

and the old-timers
took the floor
like it was their wedding dance.

I took the girl's hand
and showed her
this is all I can do
but it's what I do.

I danced her like I learned:
firm hand on her hip,
our eyes locked.
I led her with my stare,
spun her like a parasol
on my fingertips.

She arched like a guitar string
bent, slipped back,
and I held her
'til she nearly broke.

We kissed beneath the shadow of a Spanish song.

Then Grandpa and Grandma danced beside us.

He leaned in,
shouted over the music,
Hey! She's your cousin!
and danced off
like it was a secret.

But everybody heard.
Fingers pointed, young and old,
their laughing grins frozen
in the photographer's lens.

Gossip jumped the tables.
The girl ran off
and Grandpa cracked himself up.
Sorry I had to lie to you like that,
but that looked like it was going a little too far
a little too quick.
But good for you, mijo!

This moment breathes
in an old family album
in a tomb of dust.

A faded picture,
where the joyful ghosts
laugh and dance
like they will never die.

As I close the book,
an old song comes to mind.

I whisper.

All the dead desire most
is to live in our memory.
All they desire most
is to laugh and to dance.

Few people saw the bull before the ride,

its balls tied with a guitar string,

a spurred kick between the legs,

cigarette burns blistered purple as the cowgirl's hat.

She rode a white horse across the ring, bearing

the Texas flag for the national anthem.

But the whole stadium watched the bull's head snap

back as the rider held four seconds,

his leather glove glued to the reins.

The horn, curved like the heel of a boot,

crushed his face.

The cowboy inhaled his own teeth

while the bull stomped and bucked

and dreamed of the wildgrass field,

the farmer's scratch behind the ear,

the heifer it used to mount in the dark,

how Texas seemed to cover the world

like the sun.

The clowns and rodeo men emptied

their buckshots and the bull spat red clay

from its face, bit through

its own tongue, whipped its head

with the cowboy hanging from its back

like the long hair of a guitarist

who refused to stop playing

after the strings broke.

A Warning for Driving the Wrong Way

The speed limit on Mountain Road
is now eighteen miles an hour.
The stop signs on Coal Avenue are reversed.
6th Street is a two-way through downtown.
There is a construction project
on my every shortcut around this city
that seems more each day like a different city altogether.
The police officer that caught me speeding
did not expect my grandma's driveway
where it was,
and he may have heard me laughing
as my car turned and disappeared
like I was some master outlaw driver.

Which is how I feel when I run the new stoplight
at the museum that always turns red after midnight.
Or when I play chicken with the Old Town cyclists
who dress like it's the Tour de France
on the recently renamed 14th Street Bicycle Bullshit—
I mean, Boulevard,
who think traffic signs are white-privilege-optional.

I once outran a bike cop I almost killed.
Because bike cops have no lights or sirens,
how I supposed to know he wasn't going to stop
at the stop sign?

It's only while I'm driving,

that I notice how much home has changed.

How many more squad cars idle

at intersections and parking lots,

how the I-40 traffic looks like mid-90's Los Angeles,

and I feel like I'm driving the wrong way

down a road I've never been on.

I've driven past film shoots

where the studios have made Nob Hill

look like Haight-Ashbury

on one side of the street

and El Paso on the other. Even throw the Hollywood Sign

on the Sandías.

They shot the last *Terminator* in the old railyard

where the train workers union rioted

against the bosses,

which would have made a better movie

but less money.

But it's not how my late night cruises

down insomniac backstreets

shove in my face that the neighbors

are selling cheap and buying cheaper

out on the Westside,

or how fast their old homes are buried

and fresh million-dollar mansions
stand as their gravestones.

It's my recollection of the small memories,
of what used to be where,
that frightens me.
I know I've already forgotten
what to tell my grandchildren
of life before they were born.
And I will have to confess
that I can't remember.

I've always dreamt that I'll die in a car crash.
In this dream, the road decays beneath
my tires, as do the homes I pass.
In their place are freeway lanes,
fast cars, a sunset hidden by concrete.

I never see the crash,
only broken glass,
the crying driver's shadow,
the policeman's boots.

But I always overhear somebody's chill voice
swearing I was the one
driving the wrong way
all along.

I worry I will wake
one winter morning
with a phone call
that Angel froze
to death in the night.

That short mutt
Grandma took off the street
from a fireman knocking on doors,
looking for a home for this stray.

She took that dog in,
called him her guardian angel.

When she told me
how she got him,
I said I was calling
animal control.

Then she reminded me,
she took me in
just the same
and we sure as shit weren't
calling the dog catcher.

So she kept him.

I feel like that dog everyday,
content with a life

tied to the spike in the dirt,
in that big yard,
running around in circles,
chasing nothing.

Barking at nothing but ghosts.
Guarding the junk from nothing.

But sometimes he breaks the rope.

Sometimes he busts out of the yard
and fights the neighbors' dogs.

The first cold night
in December,
the rope cut
through his legs,
his dog-chest,
he escaped and battled the Pit Bull,
the Rottweiler, the German
Shepherd in the road.

I pulled him
by the broken leash
as some asshole drunk
honked and cursed,
swerved and sped by us.

Angel limped inside the house,
where Grandma would nurse
him by the fireplace,
patch his wounds,
and feed him table scraps
until the months warmed up.

I am just like that dog.
I just have to remind myself
that sometimes he breaks the rope.
Someone will feed me, love me.
Someone will cry for me.
Someone will remember me.

Ain't that the dream
for junkyard dogs like us?

My grandparents got evicted from their first house
'cuz the baby wouldn't stop crying.
Banished from their own barrio
where the railroads grew like weeds.
The steel border they never crossed, 'cuz it was like they said:
We ain't got no business in the Heights.

Grandpa almost bought a house that year,
when Albuquerque was still dirt,
bnd Grandma refused.

As if the homes she cleaned on that end of town
would stare her down when she'd pass.
She'd seen them two and three stories tall.
Seen white faces in their shadows
and she complained she never knew what time it was
'cuz she couldn't hear the trains.

Grandpa built them houses out of concrete blocks
and stuccoed, half-ass adobe, cause the foreman said
the buyers wouldn't know no difference. No down payment,
fifty bucks a month.

And Grandpa almost signed the deed…

but he noticed the sun
lashed his back fiercer
in the Heights than in the valley.

Burnt his skin to dark hide,
struck his hair gray at 26 while he stacked
bricks and mortar, until he realized his hands
were too callous to live where the trains were quiet.

But the house was on San Mateo,
and my grandma called it the Heights.

Mayor Kinney moved Albuquerque High
off Central Avenue to Indian School,
rich kids coming from the east
and the rest from the west.
Auntie moved to the war zone.
They said she moved to the Heights.
Mom got married, got an apartment by the university
but they all said she lived in the Heights.

I wonder if my grandparents ever called
for floods, or the mountains to collapse
like a train run off the rails,
and named it prayer.

It's no wonder why I hate La Cueva High School,
would see Eldorado and Manzano crushed
beneath rock. 'Cuz we still got no business there.

But if Grandpa took the house,
my family leading la reconquista de los altos.

We'd leave the beat up trucks
in the model home driveways.
Play Al Hurricane records
in the middle of the night so loud
the neighbors would be too scared to call the cops.
Let the broken engine hang from the A-Frame.
Let the slaughter pigs run the front lawn.
Leave old clothes to dry on the line.
Let the mutts bark all night.
Fire rifles on New Year's Eve,
drunk on Budweiser.
Smoke Camels, pitch the butts
in the neighbors' mailboxes.
Cook raw menudo outside.
Pray rosaries in the Hallelujah-Churches.
Steal the neighbor's cable.
Key their new cars.
Fly the golden Zia
higher than Ol' Glory.
Let our mutts fuck their purebreds.
Hell, have a matanza in the back yard.
The bloody feast of la reconquista.

But my grandparents never wanted trouble.
They found a house near the midnight trains.

Besides, they never liked the Heights anyway.

All you gotta do to join Club 27
is die at 27.
It helps if you're famous.
Maybe if you blew your brains out
like Cobain, or shot your MTV money
into all your veins
like Winehouse, or join the ranks
of Joplin, Morrison, and Hendrix by choking
on your drunk vomit, maybe then someone
will give a shit
that you're dead.

If you wanna die famous in Albuquerque,
your best bet is for a police officer to shoot you,
so you'll end up on Channel 13 News.
Maybe your snuff film will go viral
and you'll be an internet-famous corpse,
but probably some vato will shank you
while buying cigarettes
at the 7-Eleven on Central
and APD will go kill him back,
and he'll wind up being the famous one
for a minute,
instead of you.

Perhaps your demise
will be at the hands

of a jilted lover
or a jilted lover's
jilted lover,
crime of passion.
Or maybe you'll hit the barricade on I-40
and make the whole city late for work.
At least that would make a good story
for your obituary.
I have contemplated the method of my death
every night since I survived 27.

And I was scared.
That fear from when I was a boy,
when I first realized I was gonna die someday,
when I realized we're all going to hell
and I thought the devil was coming for me
that night.

I welcome his embrace
like I welcome God's.
'Cuz fuck it,
either of them
can have my tiny soul
whenever they want.
So when I'm gone,
take my body to the bosque
and light me on fire.

Let's see how many rich people's houses
I can burn down as my embers
and ashes wash into the Río Grande
where I belong,
where I came from.
And play Los Lobos
while you burn me.
Play "Saint Behind the Glass"
so everyone will cry.
I want Keith Sánchez to sing at my funeral,
Levi Romero to pray the rosary,
and I want the mass delivered by the Pope.
Francis.

'Cuz if you survive 27,
it only means you're not a rock star.

Besides, I can't die now,
I've got too much shit to do.

I was put on Earth to accomplish many things.

Right now I'm so far behind,
I will never die.

We were two children who jumped
from the slide at Tiguex Park.
Held hands so when we hit the ground
our blood became stones
on the pavement.

We spent the summer days playing
before our parents came home,
never allowed to walk the streets alone.

She told her mother I convinced her,
but I was the one who jumped with the promise
of a kiss at the top of the slide, a pyramid
of red bricks and concrete.

At the edge of 19th and Mountain Rd.
where no one was watching,
before the city statutes
and realtors scarred our neighborhood.

But it was ours still.
The streetlights hung dim
like the shadows of ghosts
dangling from their necks.
She said, *When you jump,*
the whole world vanishes for a second
except for you.
She had jumped before.

After,
on the ground,
our knees skinned
like a handful of grass
torn from the field.

This was all before the ghosts in our sleep
pulled our limbs and stretched us
into these bodies
we will die in.

Our childhood is the carving
on our knees that never healed.
Laughter and prayers
we never understood.
The dream
we never woke from
when we were young, and kissed
each other's wounds
before walking home,
and never wiped
the blood
from our lips.

En la Calle Independencia

(For Uncle Art)

We discussed Pancho Villa
outside the mercado in Juárez
over two glass bottles of Dr. Pepper
sweetened with Mexican sugar,
no straw, no ice
'cuz he knew not to fuck around
with the water in Mexico
even if it's frozen.

Outside the mercado,
la Avenida 16 de Septiembre,
street of independence,
is a stumbling brown bird
begging at the bars and newsstands

where we watch the pigeons
so fat they don't fly. They walk,
cobblestone heavy, fatter
than the birds of New York City,
with no cocky attitude.

Juárez drivers have no sympathy
for Spring Break Yanqui pigeons.

The realtor shows up
and asks for my husband
the day after my jefita's funeral.
I answer in my church clothes,
buttons undone.

She wears a business suit,
foreclosure notice in her hand.

I watched her from the window
when she walked up. The women
that usually come to the door don't dress
or move like that. Her heels stab the dirt
driveway like the spikes on the tractor
out back, where the dogs are tied and barking.

She doesn't know, Alburque is farmland
depending where you go.

She tells me our home goes up
for auction at the end of the month.
Because there's no will, no records
or paperwork, highest bidder gets the lot.
I can buy it back if I want.
But property laws don't always apply en este barrio.
I show her the backyard,
I show her what the dogs do
when I take their chains off.

Llano Stew

It was 1931,
and the broke gringos
marched to California through
the high desert.
The squatters camped
on the manito ranches.
They knocked on hacienda doors

with hands darkened
by so much soil, their skin
the shade of the gente

they begged food from.
The rancheros fed them cactus
because that's all that grew
in the summer llano.
Cauldrons of nopales stewed
with mint and lilacs.

Chunks of meat
from a dead horse's leg
bobbed in the pot

while the flies,
cuervos, and the sun
picked at the bones.

Around the campfires,
a hundred vagrants
lined up at the pots

like the breadlines
in the cities they abandoned,
like rain abandons the desert,

and took spoonfuls
into their mouths,
with tongues covered in spines.

They thanked the nuevomexicanos
and God for filling their guts
with the only abundance

the desert has for the starving:
the thorns, the dead,
and the dust.

It rained on Father's Day this year,
and as I stood in the storm,
locked outside my truck,
I remembered a story.

I heard you stood
up at Saint Charles
during my baptism

when my mother stood alone
at the altar with quiet tears
and me in her arms
as all the church ladies
whispered their righteous gossip
behind her back.

'Cuz my father never showed
at the church like he said he would,
while Grandma cast her hateful eyes
at those shit-talking crones
because she could do nothing
but stay quiet.

Was it Auntie Jeannette's jab
in your ribs that guilted you to rise
from your pew and hold me
as the priest anointed my forehead?

What made you save us?

I wondered this
all those times you bully me to fix
the plumbing in grandma's house,
or while we patch the swamp cooler,
pull weeds, haul trailers of junk
to the city dump,
or when you drive across town
to bail my ass out wherever I broke down
this time around.

I laugh while you yell at me
about my laziness and my fuck-ups
'cuz you're always right.

With that damn Jersey accent of yours,
loud as the airplane engines
you worked on in the army
back when you were my age.

Did you ever imagine marrying
into a Mexican–American family
would be so much work?

Why did you sign up for this job,
to be the workhorse for a family
who first called you gringo

but would eventually call you son?
Why do you save me every time?

I guess that's what you'll always do.

This storm didn't quit like they tend to,
and I stood in the street like a sunflower
that hasn't tasted the rain in weeks,
like a child who was never baptized,
thinking of you.

In God's eyes, you are my father
as you are in mine,

you loud, wise pain in the ass.

Lorenzo mocked his executioners
as they burned him.
The gridiron seared crosses
in his backside, and the Romans feared
he may have been a god
because he did not scream once.
There in the palace courtyard,
the governor had an African elephant
grilled over a fire pit.
The Feast of Jupiter.
All the nobility of Rome.
Their dying empire
denied no gluttony.

In the hour before, the republican guards killed
by their own swords, when Lorenzo's army of beggars
rioted at the gates.

Only the spilt cauldrons of oil
and the archers' flamed arrows
could martyr the rebellion.

The governor ordered Lorenzo stripped,
beaten, and burnt
as entertainment.

And as he burned,
the saint shouted,

Let my body be turned.
One side has broiled enough.

The crowd howled. Some drew knives
over who would first eat the ribs.

Then the soldiers turned the saint
in mercy. Bile purged
as they gagged.

Lorenzo laid until he smoldered
to bone.

His innards seared
to the gridiron, slipped from his bones
onto the white coals. They left him
until everything burned.
Loins. Chest. Face.
But his eyes remained.

A statue of San Lorenzo
sits on the altar
in the chapel Grandma built
next to the washroom.
She lit candles to him every night.

Basically, it was her way of saying,
don't be a llorón.

Saint Michael Condemns
the Bigot to Purgatory

You are no saint yet.
There will be no feast on your death day,
old man. The only candles lit for you
will burn from your wife's hand.
When you leave here you'll be forgiven.
Until then, you are waiting. There is no question
that here exists. The space between.

Here you live your failures
like waking dreams.
Here, memories burn in the spirit
until you are prepared.

Reflect now on the times you've prayed.
The first time death called. Your screams swelled
like the church bell
at your funeral,
thinking of her as you waited to die.

And you called out to me.
But I don't answer prayers;
I cut demons. Soldier angel.

You did not survive by my blessing.

You prayed for your daughter once.
Mi niña linda, you'd whisper
in her ear.

She knew your breath
from infancy, tequila kiss
on her forehead.

As a girl, she prayed silent
the nights your drunken mouth
hissed from the next room
as you broke dishes
on the wall
instead of your wife's face.

You denied her, remember, in her teen years.
That hate swelled beneath your skin
when she confessed her love for a girl at school.

When the nuns frightened her
to believe she was destined for hellfire.
And you cast her out.

That night she wept
like the virgin at the foot of the cross,
because she only chose
to serve God
and you.

Years after, cancer swallowed
her bones, the tumor bulged in her skull.
You thought it looked like a beating heart.

She never forgave you before she died
while you waited at her bedside.
Words are harder than knuckles.
Rosaries always stung
like raw salt on your tongue.
Reflect now on the times you've prayed.

That night you beat the boy
in the street with your friends.
Prove your manhood, they said.
And after, you cried
to the Blessed Mother,
prayed he wasn't dead.

Reflect now.
The morning the doctors revealed
you'd die from the same cancer
that took your little girl.

You spun restless in the hospital bed,
and the priests came at your wife's call
to chant over you, anoint your forehead,
forgive your sins
without question.
You don't know how to pray, peregrino.

So you will wait.

The gates will not open for you
until your wife joins you
in this dead place.

Stand at her side.
A crucifixion nail spiked
through her palm.

Not until you push your hand
into hers,
nail driven bone,
suffer like the Christ,
live again your pain
as you did on Earth,

only then may you rest.
But until then you will wait,
and believe,
her years will be centuries to yours.

You will know silence;
it is your name now.
You will know patience.

You will learn
to become a saint.

Johnny Tápia and Danny Romero,
two homeboys duked
it out at Caesar's Palace back in '96.
North Valley versus South Valley,
aired nationwide on HBO.
Tápia won by decision,
twelve rounds,
and a million in cash changed hands
across the city, ten, twenty,
hundred bucks at a time.
It was a long fight. Long enough to get drunk,
sober up, and get drunk again. All pissed off
when it was time to pay up
for putting your dollar on Romero.

But that night, two vatos
Johnny Montoya and Danny Lucero,
also duked it out
at the park, over a bad gamble,
and a crowd gathered,
bigger than the masses in Vegas.

Johnny cornered Danny against the swings,
dirt-sweat, bloodied faces.
Or maybe it was Johnny
on the ground

with the swing chains
around his neck.

No one could tell.
The streetlights never came on
and everybody ran at the sirens,
so no one saw who walked away
at the end.
The cops found the playground empty, except
for that body under the cottonwood.
Neighbors watched from their windows,
but they couldn't see nothing. Just dark, red
and blue lights, silhouettes.

Danny and Johnny disappeared,
just like Romero and Tápia,
along with their fame, their muscles,
and their money. Ain't no immortality
in Duranes.

Ten years later, someone carved
both their names in the old bark
of that rotting cottonwood,
In Loving Memory of Danny y Johnny,
because nobody ever knew
which one of them
was dead.

Grandpa's hands were hard
as Chevy steel 'neath a rusting '76 hood.

His truck was rusting darker than his own skin.
Oil and grit stretched over steel bones
and those eight cylinders rumbled louder than the mixer
in the brickyard at Utility Block Co.
Vicious as the boss
who signed the paychecks.

Grandpa worked himself skinny, stoic
as a saint while the bill collector worked
himself fat.
This morning still dark at 6:00,
even the bricks glowed blue
like headstones
as he inspected the cement compressor,
the iron tomb at the center of the yard.

Then someone turned on the machine
and the lights flashed orange as daybreak.
Steam rose like an angry ghost,
the cement ran red,
and the gears stripped his back
when the men pulled him out.

Three weeks in Presbyterian Hospital, two surgeries,
collapsed lung, ribs broken.

He'd joke from his bed,
The bill collector's gettin' thin
now that I'm working
out of the office.

Later that day,
the insurance man showed
with pen and paper.
The accident bailed out
everything: the medical bills,
the loans, the house.

Grandpa's blood paid off his life
and the Chevy was bought
with the air he still breathed.

Twenty years spun over
and the truck never broke down.

It only gets lazy, he said.
My truck is like me,
you make it do too much
it'll tell you, Kiss my ass,
I ain't doin' shit!

Sunday morning, he skipped church
to work in the driveway,
changing air filters, toping fluids.

He'd been looking for that damn oil leak
since Reagan got elected.
I helped Grandpa with my childhood duty:
shined the flashlight
on the dark corners of the engine
and asked, *What's that do?*
about everything he touched.

He told me again about the accident.
This time he broke a hip
and his spine,
and he climbed from the machine
with his knuckles.

Then his brother-in-law walked up the drive.

Tío stood over Grandpa,
smooth as a new Cadillac,
packed a mouthful of Copenhagen,
spat black and heavy like 10-40
when he asked,

> *How much you want for your truck?*

> and thumbed a wad of bills
> from last night's casino win.

The money stench
on his fingers.

Grandpa, grinning the rusted teeth
of a junk wrecker said,

    Just what I paid for it.

    How much is that, oiga?

Money unfolded soft as the lucky roll.
Grandpa cleared his throat like a gear grinding,

    I'll sell it for a dollar three-eighty.

    What the hell is a dollar three-eighty?

    It's nothing and it's everything, compa.

I knew a dollar three-eighty
was the price tag on your life.
And my uncle was no fool:

    So then it's not for sale, hombre?

    Not unless you got a dollar three-eighty, pendejo.

La Llorona Returns

for Tiffany Toribio,
who killed and buried her son in Alvarado Park, May 2009

Sometimes the ghosts of old legends find new life
when we speak their names.
They don't watch from the shadows
of old homes, or lurk the hallways
of abandoned hospitals.

The devil is not in the darkness.
La Llorona of legend
did not die in the waters.
She did not carve her name
in the riverbed with her fingertips,
swept away with the current,
when the Río Grande earned its name.
She began as a story
to frighten children,
the corn maiden with a Spaniard husband
who left her shamed with two sons
and returned to his other wife in Spain.
Only the cottonwoods remember,
her hair tangled in their branches.
Her children have sunken
into the mud, where the minnows and trout
turned their bones to fine sand.
Legend says she waits in the bosque
to lure the young into the waters.

But she returns in other ways.
The summer heat burns the same now as it did
three hundred years ago.
Still it makes even the strongest people snap
like cedar branches during a thunderstorm.

Last year, the news stations ran their stories,
and we learned the new Llorona's name,
but erased it from our memories
fast as we heard what she had done.
The reporters did not tell us the whole story,
only how the child's cries pulsed his mother's ears
until it seemed they were bleeding.
The cameras showed the empty playground,
the swings where they found his body,
crime scene tape and officers between squad cars.

Days later, we learned of her hands,
wisped and rough-edged as she held her son.
The boy only cried louder
the morning she was thrown out the home.
And the kid kept crying,
and nothing she did could stop him,
and the park was empty
but she swore that everyone was staring at her,
and she remembered life before the baby.

And that's when La Llorona returned.
Her hands on the boy's neck
like the sweat she would wring from her hair.
She clawed until the crying drifted.
But she stopped. Breathed
life back into her boy.
And then killed him again,
too scared of the questions the doctors would ask.
They arrested her the next day
and she disappeared.

But she reminds us that spirits
don't possess their victims with purpose.
We have created these demons.
They live in all of us.
La Llorona of legend does not only breathe
in the story or in the mind.
She lives in the water and we all drink
from the same river.

Cuete

Don't leave the house alone
when the cuetes are going off,
I was warned.
And I think of all the gunshots
hidden in fireworks
this night, the crowded emergency room
at University Hospital,
all the people too scared
to call the ambulance
or the cops.
I think of the dogs in my barrio
howling rusty with the sirens,
the black cats, and the thunderstorm.

Let freedom burn like a cuete.

I could never confess
I've always hated this holiday,
'cuz isn't every day the gringo's
independence day?

You know how many kids
got the 4th of July
on their headstones?

In his mind,
the boy Manuel's
note read:

> *Querida,*
> *I have seen you everywhere:*
> *the schoolyard; the market;*
> *the KiMo, for cartoons*
> *on Saturday morning.*
> *Riding the trolley*
> *on Central Avenue.*
> *You dance as you walk*
> *to early Sunday mass,*
> *stopping to kiss the hand*
> *of Saint Francis.*
>
> *From the last pew*
> *I stare while you twist your hair,*
> *cut short like Betty Boop,*
> *and you never catch me.*
> *I imagine you smell like the pink roses*
> *that grow in the church courtyard.*
> *The first day I heard your laugh*
> *was the day you read out loud in class*
> *and you giggled at the English words*
> *that made you sound silly.*
> *The same words*

I ran from
and never came back.
Your smile is like the sunrise
I know too well.
I work the brickyard
since I slapped that teacher.

No one would ever hit me,
tell me what to do, again.
Now I take orders
only from the boss.
My hands burn raw.

Seems like everybody
gets away with it these days.

But I see the sun over the mountains
and I think of you
as I stack bricks
ten feet high.
And I see the sun hit the mountains
and I think of you
as I walk home
with a dollar in my pocket
for each day I worked
myself closer to the grave.

I hate church
but I live for Sundays.
It's the only place I see you
anymore.

One day I'll stand
beside you during the Our Father
and take your hand.

One day I'll stand
beside you before the altar
and hold your hand.

Please, my love
tell me your name?

But the paper was chicken-scratched
with a knife-sharpened pencil
in a clumsy hand and said only,
I tink I luv yoo.

Manuel reminded himself
why he was the oldest kid
in the eighth grade.
They'd both be better off
if he just let her pass.

But the boy crumpled
the confession and dropped it at the foot

of Saint Francis like an offering.
He walked to the rosebush
while the people gathered
as Easter mass ended.

He pulled the smallest
blossom from the rosebush
and tapped on her shoulder.
When she turned
to face him,
he tossed the rose
at her feet
and he ran
like South Valley dogs
were chasing him.

The next Sunday
she found him crouched
behind the rosebush.
She was wearing a dried flower
in her Betty Boop hair,
when she told him
her name.

Rosita.

Praise the saint
who guards the space
where my grandparents met.

Praise the sunrise, the sunset,
the Sandías.

And praise the roses
that bloom every year
on Easter Sunday.

Manuel Leyba Speaks to the Bulldozer

My grandfather built this home
with bricks he cut
from the ground.

Deep below the Rio Grande,
below our homes, flows the hidden river.

He dug with a shovel,
broken handle,
until his feet were wet.
Machete-cut the bricks,
lifted them out, and shaped
the walls until his palms were smooth
with sand.
This house is terrón, not adobe
like the realtors called it.

Mamá birthed us all here.
Her godmother at her side,
la curandera burning sage
with kerosene.
The healing woman kept a dishpan
between mamá's thighs, filled
to overflow with clean water,
so we might be born floating.
Quiet as a tree caught
in the current.

The river flooded when I was young.
Pooled around our ankles
and the worms, smaller than the end
of an eyelash, found the sores
on our feet.

We warmed the home with a wood stove,
burned piñón in the cold, and smoke tangled
our hair. We carried fire with us
like shadows.

Mamá boiled our clothes clean.
She kept a fire pit in the yard.
Used a black iron puela, and the soot grew
into a skin around the metal.
Her hands worn down on the wash board
and her fingers gnarled
like cottonwood knots
as she hung clothes on the line between elms.

Papá planted yerba buena
where he buried my ombligo.
He pulled the ground up
with his finger, and dropped it, coiled
and dry like chile skin,
the mint seed at its heart.

My plant grew, became remedios,
tea, salves.

Hermanita fell with stomach pains
one night in the last month of winter.
She cried from her bed
and blew out the fireplace.

I watched her in the shadows, with a ball
pulsing beneath her belly.
Mamá broke an egg over manita's bare skin,
the yolk slid from her waist, found her ribs,
and burst where the tumor swelled.

She fed my sister yerba buena and mentolate
until she spent the night choking into the chamber pot
at her bedside, and the ball came up,
and she coughed a bulge of crow's feathers,
black blood, and bile.

She was sleeping when the sun rose.

In the spring I turned 10,
I helped abuelo plant a garden. The simple seeds:
corn, calabacitas, chile, papas, frijoles.
We dug each row, pulled
water from the acequia
that once spanned the neighborhood,

dug a ditch to the garden.
So that the water would cut right,
then left, cross each mound
until the flood.
We planted corn at the center,
with the other seeds around.

Abuelo was old by then,
but I remember his fingers.
They looked like they could snap
while he worked.
But they worked
so quickly.

He kept his thumbnail
long like a blade to prune bad leaves
from the sprouting stalks.
We worked through the sun
and Jefe moved slower with each day.
His steps grew weary; he would grimace
when he bent to the weeds.
Even his sweat dripped slower.
Each day, the years seemed to find him
older, and each night, he withered
in his sleep.

Jefe died that summer
and he didn't leave no will.
Didn't need no paper to tell
us what was ours.
We buried him
where we buried my parents
ten years later, when they fell
with pneumonia.
They all died in their beds.
I built new rooms.
Wired the walls. Installed
the plumbing myself.
I remade this house
into my own.

I met Anna at the church fiesta
when we were 20.
She wore a wine-red dress
and danced
to the mariachis.
She saw me through the crowds,
by the gazebo.
Our eyes locked.
I took her hand and we danced.

We married in the plaza
later that year.

The priest prayed the mass
and mariachis proclaimed
our marriage with horns
and guitarras.
The bridesmaids in blue.
No groomsmen.
No family to see us wed.

I got a job at the sawmill.
I ran logs through the blades
and shaped 4x10s every day
until both my hands stung with splinters
at the punch clock.

There was a joke I used to tell,
while the sweat burned in my eyes
and I breathed in the dust:
Me llamo Manuel Leyba
but they call me 'manual labor.'
Then my buddy started saying it.
Then his buddies,
then theirs.
Then the whole raza.

Anna was pregnant.
In the last days of summer, she fell
with pains in the stomach.

61

I took her to the doctors,
but they wouldn't see her.
They sent us to the clinic
on the other side of town.

Death has its modos
of letting you know.

One day I was working and Anna fell
down at the market.
The ambulance came.
No one called the mill.

Our son was born dead
as they drove.
I got to the hospital
after the phone rang at the house
and the nurse told me what happened.
The doctor said all our children
would be born dead.

Anna was silent when I brought her home.
She laid in her bed for months.
I fed her atole every day
because she ate nothing else.

We tried to make love
once but she cried and we stopped.

We never touched like that again.
Still, I loved her.
Every day I loved her.

I cradled her while she slept.
The smell of her hair while she dreamed
was the only lovemaking we needed.

I remember she got sick, slowly,
like grains of adobe crumbling
from the wall.
The doctors said it was cancer.
I cared for her
as her hair turned gray,
fine as spider's silk.

Her skin was like crumbling leaves.

I argued with the doctors to let her pass
in our home.
I snuck her out in the night,
when only the graveyard nurse was working.
The nurse never tried to stop me.

I held Anna on the porch swing.
We watched the sun fall
and she died.

That was five years ago.

The house fell apart,
and my hands now, too. The arthritis
that claimed mi abuelo's hands
has turned mine the same.

The pipes burst
in the winter.
The wires sparked
and shorted. The walls sank
with the wet ground.
Sinkholes caved in doorways.
But the work was too much
and I couldn't do no more.
Ya no puedo.

The roof leaks
on my face as I sleep.
I dream I'm drowning
every time it rains.

This ain't the first time
somebody's tried to take this house.
1955, the city came to condemn us,
but my father met them
at the door with this rifle
in his hands.

But I'm not hard like him.
Hear the sirens?
That's the chotas coming
for me.

I wouldn't have killed you, hombre.
I know you're just doing your job.
This bullet is for the man
in the suit.

But do me a favor
before they come take me.
Remember this house
after they bury it
under some fancy mansion.

It is the dirt that will cover us.
The dirt will be piled beside our graves,
our bones dug up and sold
to the highest bidder.
Nothing is ours, hombre.

Somebody else always holds the deed.

You are a Sunday mass daydream.
A Saturday morning confession.
A first holy communion crush.
You are nuevomexicana catholic delusion.

You are the girl in class
and the puppy-love-teacher-crush all at once.

I've taught myself to let you pass me by.
I know better than to chase archetypes
or girls with boyfriends.

Because I knew you'd be gone
after graduation,
just like you were gone
after la cuaresma, Easter, and confirmation
and I'd never see you again.

You're like that song I heard
on the all-night radio,
cruising the highway
in my truck.
That one song I really liked–
who sang it?

You know I never heard that song again,
but I'd know it if I heard it again.

I swear I saw you
once at the church fiestas
back when we were kids.

Maybe I heard you singing in the choir.
Or was it just your type I saw
at la posada?

You are the reason I begged my grandparents
to go to Spanish mass
even though I couldn't understand
a goddamn word they were saying.

Maybe someday we'll be saints.

You are la santa profesora
teaching that one class I never ditch
and I'm never late.

And when I catch your ear,
you never really mention
that boyfriend of yours.

Homegirl, I'm a sinner
and I don't get too many prayers
these days. So pray for me
in the dim light of the church
where I think I first seen't you,
matachine girl.

The girl I think of
as my mind wanders,
just like my mind wandered over
that first girl
back when I first liked girls.

Maybe we'll find the time
in another life.

Until then, I'll pray for you, homegirl
and thank mi tata dios
that I learned my prayers,
that I daydreamed all day in class about you,
but that I paid enough
attention in class
to know what the hell
an archetype is.

This morning, I wake
like the first breath
after drowning,
contemplate my dream
and the name
I could have given you:

Angela Ríos y Flores.
My angel of the rivers and flowers.

And when I slept last night,
my only dream was of a seraphim
floating over the Rio Grande.
Rose petals fell from
her wings and burst flames:
purple, red, blue, white, gold, and black,
as I chased her through
the brown river
that pulled me under.

And through the hazy water
I reached for her
and watched the embers burn
out on the river's face,
and on my own.

She left ripples of colored ash
on the water as she flew away.

And in my bed,
I thought it funny:
under the water
she seemed so much
closer than she really was.

I can't believe it's already February
and the air feels like April.

How long's it been since New Year's Eve?
I vaguely remember it snowed that night.

Almost certain of it.
Those pink clouds above

that giant Christmas Tree in Old Town.
You and I alone in the plaza,

even the ghosts polite enough to look away
as the two of us kissed

at midnight. There were snowflakes
on my windshield when we drove back

to my place. When we woke in the morning,
it all melted, except for a couple piles

at my doorstep. The snow doesn't seem
to stick around much these days.

You pretty little winter storm.
You leave me like a boy

praying the snow would keep coming
down a little while longer,

like maybe it could stick this time.

On Ash Wednesday

After confession, I kneel in penance
at the back of the church.
As I pray, I'm reminded of King
David and his love
for a soldier's wife.

My love, it was months
before you told me about the army boy
who thought you'd be waiting for him
after the war.
You were never mine.
so how would I have thought
we'd end any different?

I always thought he'd come after me
and I'd have to fight for you.
But you did me same as him.
No blood needed.
I remember the story well.
How the king of Jerusalem
watched her bathe.
How the clean water gleamed
from her silhouette in the daylight,
her breasts framed by the sun.

The day after you left
I moved into this room.

Left to my solitude
and my drinking;
my mess.

That studio piled
with dusty boxes,
all the shit I don't need.

I couldn't sleep.
The parking lot light
cast through the blanket
over my empty bed
on the floor.

Couldn't sleep through the rumble
of the student ghetto.
Central Avenue ghosts
can't sleep, either.

The shadow of her burned his eyes
so he could see only her while he slept.
So he had her husband killed.

You are no David
but your sin is the same,
the priest told me.
He all but damned me
over you, Angel.

The difference between me and the King
was he had the wealth.
And the life I could build you
wasn't enough. You didn't believe
in my hands. Dirty with engine grease
and ink, soil and callous,
and gentle enough
for our babies,
who would have had your eyes.

How many of your friends
asked why you wasted your time
with a grunt like me?

My friends all laughed
'cuz they always knew
you were leaving.

I treated my drinking like it was Lent.
40 days I dreamed you
in bed with the stranger
you left me for.

Fifth night of my drinking,
I saw you at the bar with him.

Saw you in every girl's eyes
after that.

The tenth night, I dreamed I was him
in bed with you
while Sam Cooke cried from the stereo.

The last night of my drinking,
I dreamed you from the concrete bed
in the jail cell.

This is where my sins have found me.
May yours find you, someday.

And as I kneel whispering Hail Marys
I've said my whole life in penance
of all the things I've done,
so I will let you go.
I have already confessed you away.
This is the final prayer.

I loved you, I love you,
I release you.
Amen.

My grandpa fought in the Mexican Revolution,
took a piss with Emiliano Zapata,
smoked a leño with Pancho Villa.
He was a veteran of WW I, II, Korea, Vietnam
He taught FDR how to cuss in Spanish.
My abuelo was a member of the United Farmworkers,
the labor union, the Chicano Movement.
He marched on Washington twice.
Won a Congressional Medal of Honor and a Purple Heart
but lost them both to Fidel Castro in a poker match.
He was a Mexican professional wrestler
known only to the world of luchadores as El Chingón:
the great-grandson of Geronimo, Apache warrior.
He was a mechanic in Al Unser's pit crew.
Played guitarrón with Johnny Cash, Marty Robbins,
and Willie Nelson.
Worked construction on the astrodome,
and once in the late seventies,
got into a bar fight with Hulk Hogan
and beat the living shit out of him.

And all this before my grandpa was 21 years old.
Well, that's what he told me.

Told me and the rest of his grandchildren as we sat,
legs crossed, circled around the recliner in the living room,
the ancient terrón mud walls of our home in Old Town.

My grandmother called him mentiroso,
a liar with a mouth vast as the mesa
that hid the sun after dark.

But he was no liar,
he was a storyteller.

As a child, his legends
played in my head as I slept,
gave me dreams I could never touch.

One night before bed, I asked Grandpa
to teach me stories
rather than prayers.

Ay, mijo, stories are prayers.
They are songs sung to the years
that you will never see.
They will hang in the ears of the young
and split their tongues
long after your breath has become the sunset.

Grandpa's words were his truth.
Testament that a beating world
flowed beneath whatever memories
the future would hold.

We sit on the floor
and listen to the time Grandpa

walked down to Old Town Plaza,
shook President Clinton's hand,
and told him a joke.

And three years later,
when he walked to the same plaza,
shook President Bush's hand,
and called him un pendejo, cabrón estúpido.
Un culo que va y toma el sudor de los huevos y las nalgas.

He swore that was a joke too.

We listened of his and Grandma's first kiss,
their hearts two stars of the desert night.

I've always wanted to tell a story like him.
He was the first poet I've ever heard
the only father I've ever known.
The storyteller.
My grandpa
was the word.

Sometimes, I wonder what stories
of his own death he's told.

Whether in his own words,
he was gunned down
on the shores of Normandy,

or in a Mexican border town
at the itchy hand of Dillinger.

Generations beyond the truth
of the hospital bed
in the living room
where his recliner used to be.

Truth in swollen bones,
gust from withered lungs.

What tales of heroics then?

When our breathing ancestors
become the soil that stains our flesh
that sunset of our skin
when we become their stories.

My grandpa was
a liar and soothsayer,
a guitarist of flaming words,
the prayer, the song, the story
that will hang from my ears,
split my tongue,
be sung from every memory in my breath.

Una Plática I Did
and Did Not Have with Tony Mares

I get drunk and stoned
and fall half-asleep on my recliner,
and Tony Mares rolls up
riding a unicorn.

He knocks on the screen door
and lets himself in.

I offer him a cup of coffee
and he says, *Hell no!*
That shit'll kill you.

I offer him a beer
and he takes it.

I offer him the recliner,
the seat of honor.

I call it The Captain's Chair,
I tell him.

And he sits.
And he listens to me
and my story about everything that happened
since I ran into him last.
At the coffee shop that last time.
It was summer.

The only reason I went to that coffee shop
was to flirt with that one girl
who worked there.

I bet you call her Whatshername nowadays!
He interrupts me.

He laughs. He knows the girl
I'm talking about. And he sits there
through my lost-love stories.

When I'm done,
the dead man tells me this:

When you get to my age,
you read the obituaries
and every once in a while,
one of your old girlfriends dies.

And you're upset.
But then your WIFE notices
you're UPSET.
And she asks you WHY you're upset.
And you KNOW you can't tell her the TRUTH.
But she KNOWS when you're lying.
And she's VERY curious
why you're so SAD
every couple months.

What do you tell her
when she asks you that?

Damien, you better start planning
for that situation
since now. If you do,
you will weather all storms.

Then Tony Mares gets up and walks out my door.
But the unicorn has wandered off somewhere.

He heads down the alley, past that one bar
'cross from the University,
used to be Jack's back in his day.

I offer him a ride in my truck, *Hey Tony!*
I'll take you wherever you're going!

But he yells back,
You can't go where I'm going yet.

He becomes a shadow
in the streetlight.
And I glance over at the crosswalk,
at the procession of honking cars
and screaming drivers,
and there's a fucking unicorn
blocking traffic
on Central Avenue.

In San Antonio,
the Texans flew their flags at half mast
the afternoon you died
then raised them back
the next morning.

In Albuquerque,
the New Mexicans
played your songs on the radio
and shot tequila in your name.

The pick-up trucks
with Mexican flags and cowboy hats
painted on the rear window
rolled Pacific Avenue,
bumping "¡Guacamole!"
like it was Reggaeton.

The evening news
praised the name you chose
and the Journal read,
Country Music Loses a Legend.

The old folks
across the street played
your 45s on the porch
and danced how they did
on their wedding day.

Hell, you might have
played their reception.

But the record skips
and the speaker cracks
dust like a eulogy
echoed in an empty church,
where the choir
is a lone accordion
playing one note.

You, sixteen years old
in the saloon in Lubbock
playing Buddy Holly
to drunk honkies
who didn't seem to notice
the only thing in the bar
browner than you
were the bottles of Lone Star.
Mexi-fro on your head
like a prickly pear
atop a cactus.

You took the name of your guitar
as your own.
Slung it over your shoulder
like a 30-30 rifle

and sang country
like Pancho Villa
raising hell
across the border.
You called it Tex-Mex.

"I'll be There
Before the Next
Teardrop Falls"
is rumored responsible
for my mother's conception,
and there isn't a nuevomexicano
who doesn't know the words
to "Hey Baby, ¿Qué Pasó?"

Lovers done wrong
scrape their snakeskin heels
on the VA dance floor.
Kiss while you sing them
a cowboy song in Spanish
from the jukebox.

You got caught smoking grass
by the Dallas PD,
spent a year in the pinta,
dreamed Johnny Cash
would break his guitar

over the warden's head
and rescue you to Nashville.

But Freddy, no one cared
the morning you died.

The flags hung limp at full staff,
the AM Country Station was silent,
and the pick-ups wouldn't start.
My guitar fell in the night
and the new strings broke
in the case,
never played.

El Soldado Razo

At the cemetery in Santa Fe,
a dust storm browned the sky
as they lowered the old man in the grave.
The tombstone already cut with his name,
a photo from his days as a boxer
framed in marigolds.

The priest laid a gold crucifix
on the casket, draped with the American flag,
red and white roses,
his Purple Heart.
Everything covered in dirt.

The soldiers readied their rifles,
white-gloved and straight.
No one will remember their faces.

The family recited, Amen,
seven guns drawn
in salute.
First shot fired.

I imagined him in a cadets bar,
weeks after Pearl Harbor.
The barfight champion,
he stood short,
thin mustache,
cocky smile.

And the Texan heaped on the floor
couldn't remember shouting wetback,
or the beating
that caught the staff sergeant's attention.
Seeing that Sarge was the boxing coach,
he gave my uncle a new name.

Peewee was a featherweight after that.
He didn't bring the hardest punch,
but he was fastest they'd seen.
Soon army trophies, gold gloves, and photos
of his fist in the air
filled the mailbox back home.

Second shot. Seven rifles.

June 6, 1944.
French shoreline.
Hollywood put John Wayne and Eastwood
on the beaches, silver screen legends
and fake war heroes.

But the first waves of D-Day
also had ships cramped
with Black, Indian,
and Mexican platoons.

Perfect targets
for the Nazi gunmen,
and that shit ain't in no movie.
He was machine gun-ripped
shin to shoulder.
One buddy fell face-down.
Then another.
Then thousands.

Peewee lay like a corpse.
How many bullets stitched his side?
Saltwater foamed
and crusted his wounds
as the tide came in.

His prayers were in Spanish.

Third round. Final shot.
The glories of battle didn't earn much respect
back home. The next 20 years left Peewee
with German lead in his hip
and he limped the street
when the bartenders exercised their Right
to Refuse Service.

He never boxed again,
except for that pickpocket
in the grocery store parking lot.

A few years back, some vato
stole his social security check and ran.

But Peewee hooked his cane around the punk's leg
and gave him everything.
One shot for the war.
One for dishonor, the insult
of coming home
to the same 'ol America he bled for.

One shot for every bullet he took.
Next day, he made the news.
A hero.
Only time his name inked the paper
except for the obituary.

Soldiers fell into rank
as the casket lowered,
but this was not the only time
my uncle died.

They killed him once
on the shores of Normandy;
again, rejected in his homeland,
el soldado razo; and again
in the old folks home.
Babbling senility,
a lonely, soiled bed

where the glory of death was a
a cruel hoax.
After the funeral, Old Glory
waved at the cemetery gate
as it should.

But as the sun broke through the dust
it burned the flag.

For a moment its colors
were red, blue,
and brown.

Johnny,
did you die the way you wanted to?
Did you want the mystery?
Everybody arguing
about what finally killed you.

It was the pisto.

Nah, the method.
La coca.

Or was it the pills the doctor gave you
to kill the phantoms
of chingasos,
la vida loca?

But you wanted to die
in the ring.
A knockout punch to break
your neck.
Proof.
The only way
to beat your ass
was to kill you.
La muerte,
the referee.

Did you see yourself
laid out on the canvas?
Flashbulbs and cameras
swarming your body
like flies. Your teeth covered
in red spit, photographed
in black and white.
The cover shot
on all the sports magazines.

Your dead face plastered
on them all.
Or did you see yourself
in the cajón
at twenty-one years?
Some vato's switchblade
or bullet
in your chest
or your throat?

Nah, you wanted to die like a cholo.
A homeboy's funeral. A mile of lowriders
trailing your corpse
on way to the camposanto.

Or did you see yourself
an old man?

Grandkids at your feet
hooked on all your stories:
Glory and championships;
legends of all the guys
you knocked out.
The title belts
and your trophies.
Would they want to be you?
Would you let them dream such dreams?
And would you tell them the truth
about everything?

Johnny,
how many of us
barrio children pretended
to be you
in our best schoolyard
fistfights? Imagined the playground
Caesars Palace, the crowd of kids
celebrities at the ringside.
We knew we'd be famous someday
if only we'd never lose.
But we always lose.
We knew it back then.
And in the end
you lost too, vato.

All you proved
beating Danny Romero
is that Burqueños love
beating the shit out of each other
almost as much as we love
beating the shit
out of ourselves.
Yet you were still our hero.
We got drunk
in the parking lot
at your memorial.
And tonight we celebrate
you in your city. A santo
with the devil horns
holding up the halo.
As we move on,
we ask what finally did you in.

Wonder what you could've done
if only you had more time.
Wonder what you're up to
on the other side,
'cuz you always left us
wondering, bro.
Always wondering.

El primer

I dreamed this all.
The morning my mother died,
I saw her in the emergency room bed.
Curtain pulled back,
her shirt torn where the doctors cut,
defibrillator burns on her chest,
breasts exposed,
a plastic tube taped to her mouth.
My stepfather slouched in the chair
beside her, my grandparents
praying over her.
The stroke left her burning
for 30 days.

I dreamed this all to life.

La segunda

How the holier-than-thou ladies
at church wept when they learned
my mother died
without the last rites.

You must take care
of your soul at all times,

the catechism teacher
warned the class
when I showed up late
for the last time
the next Sunday.
The God they taught me
was not the same God
we prayed to in my home.
The God of the dirt
and the river and the corn
was God of all things
and He would not have
my mother suffer more
than she did.
Would her hell
be life relived?
Would her face be forever bruised
into knots from my father's fists?
Would she be working
three jobs 'til Jesus comes?
Would she look into whatever
mirrors are in eternity
and always see her face
how she never wanted to be remembered:
wrinkled and fat, paralytic, slumped,
so swollen

she couldn't even cry?
She'd already burned,
and the God I knew
knew this also.

My mom's not in hell,
I whispered, as I walked
out of Saint Mary's.

I'd grown used to the pity
and the stupid things
people say when they don't know
what to say.
That poor girl at school
who empathized. She knew exactly
what I was going through
grieving her dog
that summer.
I sat in my room
in those days after, all pissed
that everyone was feeling sorry
for me instead of themselves.
But I guess we're all gonna burn someday.

El tercero

We found an owl in the basketball hoop
in the backyard a week ago.

Grandma wanted to kill it,
a bad omen
that needed to be handled.
A demon sent
by someone with a grudge.

Its bloody shit stained the driveway,
trapped in the net like a nightmare
in a dream catcher.
But my stepfather
let the owl live.

He buried his superstitions as a boy
when he buried his mother
after a Dead Man's Curve crash
on Isleta.

Bullshit, I thought I heard him say
as he climbed the ladder.

The owl clawed him
when he cut it down.
Grandma blessed his bleeding hand

with holy water
then doused the bird.

It locked its eyes into hers
and hissed.

El cuarto

I locked my bedroom door
with the rusty hook latch.
Not like anyone would bother
me anyway.
My Grandparents mourned
by keeping silence in the house,
so I searched their shelves
for dusty books.
I found *Última* this way.
Second edition, ink drawings
of La Curandera and her boy
scattered between the chapters.
The golden carp.
The good owl.
Las hermanas brujas.
The good magic, cures
of herbs and prayers.

Hours I spent on my bed
in the dim light
of a broken lamp,
looking for answers.

Última
means the last one.

My family lived this.
I learned many families
like mine, lived this.
And there aren't many of us
like there used to be.
Some nights I'd stay up long past 2:00
in the morning.
I was always a slow reader.

El quinto

The night of the rosary
was the first time
I ever sat in the front row
of a church.
San Felipe was full,
familia en frente,
neighbors and friends
huddled in back.

And I knew they were all watching
me. Peering around shoulders
to steal a pitiful look.

I scared them
because I couldn't cry.
I sat as the Brothers of the Good Shepherd knelt
around the casket.

White-robed,
they sang el santo rosario.
It was the song of my grandmother
kneeling at her bedside,
praying to el santo niño
for all of us.

The harmonies filled
the church like candlelight
and I closed my eyes.

I felt the presence of a boy
beside me. He whispered me the words
before they came,
so I sang like I was expected to.
I did not open my eyes,
because I was afraid
he'd be gone
if I tried to look.

And I wished I could disappear
like my visions did
whenever somebody
gave me that sorry look

and their faces hardened
like those saints
in the nichos of that church,
because I snuffed myself out
on the altar,
or something like that.

Through closed eyes, I heard
that nowhere-boy's little voice:

Tienes fuerza.
tienes poder.
tienes bendiciones.
Todos los tenemos.
Nunca te olvides.

La Salve Regina

At the funeral,
I gave my mother's eulogy.

I don't remember what I said.
I remember the pallbearers struggling

to lift her casket from the hearse.
I remember the long line
of people who shook my hand
as they placed flowers in her grave.

I remember trembling as I spoke.
I remember that night,
I finished the book
and wrote my first poem.

Ten years gone now,
I stand at Calvary Cemetery
this seventeenth day
of February,
to remember you, Mama.

And I can't help
but think of the weeks
alone in my room
with my book,
the angry blood
I'll always have.

That I'll always be prepared
to lose everything
and build it all again.

We are the curanderos
who know only
how to heal ourselves.

Bless me, Mama, I am a poet now.
Look at what I've done.
Look at all I've done.

Damien Flores hails from nowhere but Albuquerque, Alburque, the Duke City, El Duque, La Plaza Vieja, La Ruca, Old Town, New Mexico, United States of Atzlán.

He earned his degree in English and Chicano Studies from the University of New Mexico, and was recipient of the Lena Todd Award for creative non-fiction from the UNM English Department.

He was named NM Hispano Entertainer's Association's Poet of the Year in 2007 and 2008. He has performed for TEDxABQ, and across the country as a key member of 10 poetry slam teams, including four national champions: ABQSlams 2011 and 2016 (National Poetry Slam Group Piece Champions), and UNM Loboslam 2006 and 2008 (College Unions Poetry Slam Invitational).

Rose Perez and her grandson

His poems appear in two chapbooks, *A Novena of Mud* and *El Cuento de Juana Henrieta*, published by Destructible Heart Press. His work has been featured in *Bomb Magazine*, *The Daily Lobo*, *Duke City Fix*, *El Palacio*, *Albuquerque: The Magazine*, and *An Underground Guide to Alburquerque*, and anthologized in *Malpaís Review*, *De Veras: Young Voices From the National Hispanic Cultural Center*, *The 2006 National Poetry Slam Anthology*, and *A Bigger Boat: The Unlikely Success of the Albuquerque Poetry Slam Scene*.

He teaches at The University of New Mexico and the Native American Community Academy, and hosts the Spoken Word Hour, Sunday nights on 89.9 KUNM-FM.